Under Our Skin

What's On the Inside is Better Than the Outside

Justine Stenneth
12 Years Old

ISBN: 978-1-77277-012-4

PUBLISHED BY:
10-10-10 PUBLISHING
MARKHAM, ON
CANADA

Contents

I dedicate this book to my mommy and daddy,
who I love with all my heart.

Acknowledgements

I would like to thank Meir Ezra for inspiring me and teaching me what I don't learn at school. I would like to give a huge thank you to my parents. Thanks to my mommy for bringing me up with an open point of view and my daddy who always told me to be myself. I would also like to thank my sisters Vanessa and Tasha who make my family complete. I have grown to appreciate how important they are in my life.

I would also like to thank Raymond Aaron and Vishal Morjaria, who helped me achieve my dream of writing and publishing a book.

Foreword

It is time for change. Are you ready? Then wait no longer and start reading this book. Justine has a purpose and she wants to contribute to improving the next generation. She believes that if only those her age could all agree that all people are good, the future would be radically different.

Her book is interactive. In one hand you hold the book, and in the other you hold pen and paper. And probably the most important action is what happens as you act on what is described in her book. It's time to take action. No more sitting around hoping that the world will get better. The energy behind this 12 year old, and the courage to take on what she believes, is very commendable.

Take a look at how she dreams the world to be, and be part of the change.

I highly recommend this book for others Justine's age, as well as those of us older than her. Together change can happen.

Raymond Aaron
New York Times Top 10 Best-selling Author

Chapter 1
Stay Positive

Hi Readers

This chapter is about staying positive, and how to know when somebody is not feeling good. My book is about not discriminating against people just because others think they are different. It is also about giving yourself power and being yourself.

When you let things happen to you and think you cannot change anything, your life will never look any different. You have a choice right now. But when you don't make the choice to be in control of your life you are at effect in your life. When you are at effect you only have reasons, excuses and when you are too busy having excuses change cannot happen. You might have a book of excuses! I know, if you are sitting behind this book, you are ready for change and you are ready to give up your book of excuses. And that's awesome! I am so happy that people are ready to make changes. If only all the people realized that living from a place of power is a much better way of living, the world would be so much different. And that excites me! Trust me; you will see how different your life can be once you are in the driver's seat. I know this book will make a difference. It is my goal that this book will change how teenagers my age see the world. I want to make a difference in A LOT of lives. And I know your life can be different. All I ask while you are reading this book is to stay open. Stay open to the idea that things can be different. That has to be the starting point BEFORE you can make any other changes. And to do that you have to stay positive.

Just know that if you are at effect you have no time for change. When you spend your time blaming you cannot make change. I feel it's not good being at effect. When you are at effect you think more about how you will make an excuse for not getting something done. The opposite of being at effect is being at cause. When you are at cause in your life you hold a belief that you have the power to make things go the way you want them to.

I will give you an example. If you have to do a book report by a certain date, and it's the day before and you haven't done any of it, your mind will say "I'll just make up a reason. I'll tell the teacher 'oh something happened and I couldn't get it done.'" You have no time to change yourself. You have no time to think 'oh I did something bad.' So instead you just make an excuse, and by doing that things never get done, including your book report.

Every time you lie or make up an excuse, you actually stop growing. I'm being dead serious with you guys –

it makes your insides go "Oh I don't want to lie" but you force yourself to.

It's like keeping something contained, like keeping a butterfly in a jar. It will eventually die, and that's how far you will be driven too. Not to death, but you guys will be the people who make up excuses for everything and you will end up feeling bad and not even realizing it. And when you live your life like that you aren't really living; that is why I say it is like death. So you have the choice to be however you want to be, but you can decide how you are going to be at any moment in time.

So if you decide to lie, others will not be able to trust you with an issue because they know you've lied before. It would be hard to trust someone who lied to me. I won't trust someone who lied to my friends. But you can always change. And that is the good news. And you can change in a moment of time.

You can change yourself to be someone who does not lie. I would love to be friends with that person who did whatever they had to in order to change. And I know everyone has it in them to not lie because I know everyone has good in them. Trust me, even if you don't believe that is me - that girl doesn't know what she's talking about - it's called being at effect.

Let me tell you there is a better way and it's called being at cause. And you have the choice to make: Do you want to be effect or cause? Before you can answer let me give you a good explanation of both.

Cause is when you have results and are in your own personal power. You can create anything you want when you are at cause. And if you read more into my book you'll see I have a chapter on keeping your power. When you're at cause you can keep your power. You can create anything. I'm telling you when you are at cause you have results. When people come up to you with their issues and actually trust you, you will have friends and people that you can trust. And you tell the truth. You tell the truth about everything.

I don't know about you but I'd like to be at cause in my life. And there are some times that you lie to somebody - and I too have lied - but you know what you have to do – come clean with them because every time you tell a lie your hands get dirty. Not physically. But you have this history that you carry around with yourself. So the way to clean your hands is to tell the truth. Throughout the book I am going to present you different challenges and exercises to do. This book isn't about just reading and not taking action. And every challenge is meant to rock your life. Every time you decide to do something better your life will get better. READY?

ARE YOU READY?

CHALLENGE ONE

Tell the truth to everyone you've lied to or made excuses to. It might take a long time to get your hands clean but it will be worth it. I guarantee that you will feel much better when you do that. If you think that is too hard you could also write it down and then rip it up. The important thing is that you take a look at what you've done. Once you've done that the next time something comes up that is the same you will stop and think "Oh I am choosing something different this time. And it feels awesome!"

Being at effect is not fun. Some people must think "oh I'm not at effect" but you don't even know you're at effect. That how bad it's gotten. Just know that being at effect doesn't help you. It doesn't help anybody. It doesn't make anybody feel okay. You'll be seen as this person with so much history. I wouldn't want to be friends with someone with a history of lying and trust issues.

You cannot create when you're at effect. When you are at cause you can create. Now I really really want you to know how important and exciting it is when you are at cause.

Let's take me, for example; do you think that if I was at effect I could have written a book? Absolutely not! But I am at cause so of course I can create. So I can create a book and then learn from my own book. If people make negative comments about it, I won't take it personally. It's their choice if they want to be negative about stuff. But being negative is being at effect. Making fun of people is being at effect. Being at cause is the best.

LET'S TALK ------
CREATE YOUR LIFE

We will be doing an exercise that gets you thinking beyond how you normally think. Let's go…..

Let's say, for example, you want to create something.

Let's say you want to build something; a chair, perhaps. If you are at effect could you make a chair? NO. You could try but it won't work. But when you are at cause the chair will be magnificent and be more than you thought. It will be over the top. And so many people would love to be friends with someone like that. You'd be trusted. And let me tell you you CAN create anything that is inside your head.

So take that as an example that you can do anything in your life that you want to do. It doesn't matter if the world doesn't like it. What matters is that you like it. Do you think everyone is going to like my book? Probably not. Do you think I'm going to be mad about it and let it eat me up inside and let people push my buttons? Definitely not. I'm not going to let anyone push my buttons. I'm not going to let anyone affect me. There are times when people eat away at you and get that little part of you that gets you irritated. That happens to me sometimes. But we all need to fight through it. Because everyone is better than what people say. Just don't care what others people say because their opinion doesn't matter if it is something you like. If it is something you like, you will have success in yourself. Believing in yourself is the way that you can stand in your power. That's how powerful cause is.

So what do you want to create?

_____

_____

_____

_____

_____

_____

Write down your thoughts about how you can create
it. Notice what positive words come out. Also notice
if you think something negative.

_____

_____

_____

_____

_____

_____

_____

_____

_____

_____

_____

_____

_____

TIP: Remember it is ALL a choice.
Right now you can decide.

Chapter 2
Don't Judge

When you judge somebody it lowers both your self-esteem and their self-esteem. Judging someone else is just as bad as saying bad things about yourself. Judging another person actually hurts you just as much as it hurts them. Because you might not know it but people have this energy around them, and you can sense if a person is having a great day, or not having a great day. Or if a person is mad or happy.

Just the way you hold yourself, the way you walk around, and the way your facial expressions are can determine how you feel or what emotions you are feeling right there in that moment.

When you judge someone it doesn't make you feel better, does it? I know that when you judge someone you might not feel it but consciously –like you are not aware of it – but it actually makes you feel worse about yourself. And what's the point of judging someone? You never know if that person that you might have called fat is starving themselves or that person that you pushed down the hallway might have been abused at home. So why do people do these things? Judging or physically abusing people is not good at all.

When I walk down the hallway at school and I can hear judging, I can't help but wonder how the person who is being judged feels.

Would you like it if someone was judging you? If you knew someone was making fun about you behind your back would you like that? I do not think that you would. Of course you know that it would make you feel bad about yourself. If I stood in a room and asked someone to say negative things about you, your level of self-esteem would go down in an instant. If you judge someone, they know it, just as you know when someone is judging you.

Ever since I was very young, I've thought -- why judge anyone? Why judge someone because of their skin colour or how they look? I'm focusing my story on skin colour because that's how my experience has been created. And because I have that viewpoint I am writing my book from that viewpoint. It's not what's on the outside; it's what is on the inside that counts.

Let me ask you two very serious questions:

1. Do YOU judge people?
2. Why do you judge people?

If you are judging someone because of their skin colour, why does that matter? Ask yourself why are you judging them because of that, because if we were all made the same – the same personality – we all looked the same and we walked around without any smiles, this world would not be interesting. I don't know about you but I wouldn't want to live in a world where we all looked the same. The world is unique because we all look different.

As I said previously, you don't like it when others judge you, so don't judge them. When you judge others you are on the effect side. Remember that, when you are on the effect side you have reasons and excuses for what you are doing. When you are on the cause side you have results and you get answers and ideas, but when you are on the effect side you don't get anything. You are not willing to change yourself when you judge other people. The biggest reason you judge others could be to make yourself feel better. But really when you judge someone you are just being as bad as you perceive them to be. And you're on the effect side. You don't know how much it really hurts you when you are on the effect side because your life is being shut down every time you say a bad word about someone.

Here is an example: Let's say you really wanted to be on a TV show but you gossip or judge others. There is a barrier that is put up every time you judge people that will not let you go to the next level. That's why it's so important to be on the cause side. That's the message I'm trying to get across. Because when you are on the cause side you can get so much more done. When you are on effect side you can't do anything. You are not willing to change. And I know there are people out there who will not be willing to change themselves but that's their problem. If you can be the person who is on the cause side you will make this world a better place. People will say "Oh that person is receiving so much." You need to carry on if someone says bad things about you, but at the same time it's important not to say bad things about other people.

It only hurts you when you make fun of other people. It doesn't make you, or the other person, feel good. But what you probably don't know is that is actually bullying. You don't want to be known as the gossiper. If you talk about someone behind their back you might think "Oh I'm not doing something bad behind their back because they can't hear it," but it is actually bullying. Or if you judge someone or tell them they are not good enough it is also a type of bullying. I do not believe in bullying. You might think this girl doesn't know anything - that's not bullying. If you don't want to believe me that's okay; I won't take it personally. That's another thing I also want to talk about. When someone judges you and you take it too personally I don't think it's okay. You can be a sensitive person – like me – I'm such a sensitive person if someone talks badly about me or gives me a dirty look, or makes it not feel happy to be around them, I might react by asking if my hair okay or if I look okay. But actually I say to myself "What does it matter what anyone else says to me?" because I am the only person that matters. That's why it's so critical when you make fun of others or judge someone that you know that it's a type of bullying. I know you don't want to be known as the person who bullies because I know I certainly don't want to be known as that person. If those people are not willing to change – as I said before, changing yourself just because of something someone else said is wrong. But in this case if you are changing yourself for the better, it's better.

I don't want you to get confused but if you are changing yourself it could be in two different ways. If you are changing yourself in a way that you're not making fun of others it is a good change, but if you are changing yourself because of the bad things other people say about you but you liked yourself before, it is not a good thing. I really want this message to get across ..... because if you guys know that when one makes fun of people it's bullying then I would be so happy because my one dream is to tell people that they do not need to be scared anymore, and they can come out for who they really are. I'm saying that if you like doing bad stuff, it's not going to help anyone, and you are probably only going to get into trouble. And worse than when other people lie is when you lie. It puts a block in your education or whatever you really want to do. It's only hurting you, not the other people who don't lie, and who are willing to change themselves for the better. Don't get those two confused; changing yourself because of what someone else says about you is not good. Don't let someone else affect you. Don't let someone else take power over you. When someone takes power over you, you lose your power and they gain the power that you had.

CHALLENGE

If you judge others, STOP it. And replace it with saying positive things to people.

Write down what happens over the next week when you stop judging.

_____

_____

_____

_____

_____

_____

_____

_____

_____

_____

Tell me what happens. Reach me on Instagram at under_our_skin because I really want to know. This is why I wrote this book so people our age can grow up totally different.

Chapter 3
Be Yourself

Do not change who you are just because of what someone else says. You are amazing! You are being you because you are awesome. And you feel like you can do anything, like you are on top of the world. When you change yourself you feel like other people will look at you differently. They don't. Being yourself is better than being anybody else. I know that every person out there is awesome just being themselves. I know you might be thinking "This girl just does not know my problems." A few months ago people were calling me weird, and I said "Whatever; it doesn't affect me." I didn't want to change myself because someone said I was weird. I just twisted that around and said "Oh, I'm weird? That's good, because weird is just another word for unique or limited addition." Technically you wouldn't want to be boring like everyone else who wants to change themselves, so just twist the words around. I know that everyone out there is amazing. Please don't change yourself.

Like I was saying before, you guys are amazing just the way you are. Everyone is amazing just the way they are. And it is important to remember that you are great. Know that being yourself is just great. You people who are reading this book are willing to sit here and read my book – and I know you are because you're gotten this far – knowing that you are yourself is an awesome feeling. It's amazing! It makes me feel so empowered. Being yourself is strong because what if people don't like you? Well, there is a person out there who is feeling just like that; maybe he or she is reading this book. Even if some people don't accept who you are, you shouldn't let that stop you because there are lots of people who are saying "These girls shouldn't do this, these girls shouldn't do that." What I say to those people is that they are just too scared to do it themselves, so of course they have to judge others. It makes me feel so sad that people judge people. If you know you are yourself you can be in your own skin and feel good about it.

Like I was saying before you need to remember that you are great. But also you have to learn to be strong within yourself. Just remember that it only matters what you think about yourself. It doesn't matter what others are saying about you. If someone else says you're useless or no good, well, that's what they think. It's only hurting themselves when they say that to you. By you thinking that it only gives them more power. So you have to remember you are the only person that matters. When it comes to thinking about what you should wear to school, you might think this person might not like it. Why are you taking into account what they might think? It only matters what you think. I know when I've gotten dressed for school, sometimes I was thinking that someone might not like it, but I realized it only matters what I think. And I said to myself `Why should it matter what others think?" It also happens when I go shopping with others – "Oh, what do you think?" It doesn't matter what others think about you. That's why that song by Taylor Swift that says "shake it off" is so powerful, because you are just going to shake it off and the haters gonna hate, hate, hate. What does it matter? It doesn't matter. That song is so powerful because she doesn't care what others think. Only what she thinks. That's why I love her as an artist.

Like I was saying it doesn't matter what others think. Don't let other people stop you from doing what you love. For example, I'm only 12 and I wrote this book. Some people might say this book is awful; would that stop me from doing what I love? NO. Are you kidding me?! That just got me more motivated to do this awesome book that can change people's lives. I am telling you from my heart, if you guys can get this message it would make me so happy. It makes me so sad that people shut people down and say "You can't do that" and the person says "Oh I won't." You know you shouldn't say I won't; it should give you more encouragement to do it even more and show them how to do it. Because you know it doesn't matter what they think. Do not let them stop you. You can do anything. How many 12 year olds can say they have written AND published a book? Not many. I put a lot of time and effort into this and I can tell you it wasn't always easy but I loved every minute.

I know I was talking about not letting anyone stop you. But also I'm going back to the point I said about not changing yourself. I tried to change myself before and thought it would be better. The truth is it's not going to be better. I really want to get this across. I would love it if you guys really know it would not be worth changing. So my experience was – I was told I was weird. I used to call it crazy hours on Christmas when I used to be crazy. So when I was told I was weird and I took it as a good thing. I thought it was a compliment. I got called it so much it made me feel unique. It made me feel like I was not the same as others. I hope my story really helps you take any situation and make it into a good one.

Like I said before, you can take a bad situation and turn it into a good one. You are the only person who can make you feel a certain way. No one else. If you let anyone else come in between, it will not be good. If you let them do it that is not good because that's when people get bullied. Stand up and let them know. My mom always tells me "They cannot make you feel any way without your permission." I think this is the best thing my mom ever told me. You get how powerful that is? By letting someone make you feel a certain way you are giving them permission to hurt you. Do you want to give them that permission? A lot of people have hurt me in the past. After that I thought"Oh my gosh, that person has taken advantage of me and I'm letting them win." It's like that belief that dogs can sense fear. So you don't want to get scared like when a dog comes near you? It just makes you even more scared and the dog picks up on it. Sometimes people push your buttons to make you feel a certain way. I want to let you know you can use your words to stand up for yourself and make your life better. You don't want someone taking advantage of you. I hope that helps you know what to do when someone is pushing your buttons.

CHALLENGE: BE YOURSELF

This has to happen BEFORE anything else. So start off in the morning and look in the mirror and say "I love me just the way I am." Even if you want to change something in your body like your muscles or weight you have to love yourself FIRST.

Exercise: EVERY TIME you are in front of a mirror say "I love me just the way I am." How does it feel to do this? Notice how it gets easier with practice.

_____

_____

_____

_____

_____

_____

_____

_____

Chapter 4
Keeping Your Power

When you have power you can do anything. Have you ever had that moment when someone said something nice to you or you had a realization that "I did that so perfectly." In that moment you feel like you can do anything. You have to keep that moment at all times, even when you don't feel good about yourself. Just think about that time when you felt like you could do anything. I've had those moments a lot. Before I wrote this book I wasn't sure I could do this, or how could I possibly do it. But in that moment of realization that this is actually happening - when I started writing and it was happening - this is the moment like I feel I can do anything in my life. It's true; ever since I was a little girl I had so many options about what I wanted to do. I wanted to help people. Helping people is one of my best things. And getting the message across that says when you have your power you can do anything. Imagine if everyone had that feeling all the time. Do you know how powerful that would be if everyone had that? This world would be so different - so kind and so nice. When someone does something bad to you, don't do it back to them because it takes your power away at that time. When you have your power you feel good, like you can do anything. It's true. This world may have some corruption but remember you need to keep your power and things will be awesome.

As I said, you can do anything when you have your power. But you also have to remember how you hold yourself. IF you walk around all hunched over and scared that something might happen you will be a target for a bully. You need to be able to walk around proud. You know in the movies when people say walk around like a princess you think straight up and proud, head up? I do that all the time and people say "wow." And I'm very tall for my age too, and I still walk straight. That's what you need to do – walk around proud.

You need to do is walk around so people say "wow." I love it when people do that because they walk around in their power. Everyone can have their own strength. We don't have to be good at everything. Because if we were perfect we wouldn't be on the earth. The earth is made for people who make mistakes and learn from those mistakes. Heck, I learn all the time. When you walk around proud it makes you so happy. Everyone can walk around proud. It makes me feel so good to see that, because I know these people are feeling good. These people know inside they are the best because it only matters what is on the inside. The outside doesn't matter. It is very important to walk around proud every day.

Remember how I was saying when you judge someone you are on the effect side? It's true. But when you are keeping your power and you are telling people how good they look, you are on the cause side. You have result from that. Your life will be so much better if you just stay calm and keep your power so you can do anything. If you walk around proud and give people a simple thank you it will make your day. Some people walk around and, for example, in a fast food restaurant they take their food and just go, and are all angry. You don't have to do that. And when you are in the grocery store and you thank the cashier, it makes you and the cashier feel good. If you walk around with negative energy, you will never get anywhere. If you walk around being proud, people will see you have a positive energy around you. And if you feel like doing good you are on the right path. People who do good do succeed. It doesn't mean a big house or riches; if you doing good to others you are helping the world and are wealthy in all ways.

IDEA

By you doing good you are helping the world. It is registering in your brain that you are doing good, have power and are helping the world. Here's another thing –

I call it the Power Theory.

This is how the Power Theory works:

Let's say your mind thinks "I'm not smart" or someone says that you are not good. You have to take it and twist it around so you say "Oh ya I am smart." Then your mind will click every time you do something and your mind will think "I'm doing a good thing. I'm smart." That's why it's so powerful. Let's say you're mixed – you might not think you're not good because the terms are black and white. Let's say you think you're not good because you're black. You need to register in your mind that you are unique and it doesn't matter what your skin colour is. It's just a skin colour. If we had the same skin colour the world would not be unique. I wouldn't want to live in a world where everyone looked the same. I love all cultures because of the different skin colours. So don't judge people because of their skin colour. That's why my theory is important. If your mind can register and say "Ya, i'm doing something good" and your mind can click, that's how you keep your own power.

The power theory is all about taking action. If you do not take action how will you be able to change? And if you aren't able to change yourself you will be on the effect side. If you are willing to change yourself and take action by using the power theory, you are on the cause side. Also taking action is about standing in your own power. It's aboutbeing yourself. It's also about staying positive. Taking action is all these things.

CHALLENGE - So just do it!!

Use my Power Theory every day.   A good time to use it is when you notice you are saying things to yourself that are not good.

Write down how you change it around.

_____

_____

_____

_____

_____

_____

_____

_____

_____

_____

_____

_____

_____

Chapter 5
Do not Discriminate

This is the most important chapter because the subject is so critical. This chapter is about discrimination, and how not to discriminate based on skin colour or any other factor. If people would stop judging others based on their skin colour, or their outsides or religion, this world would be so much better. I will talk about skin colour because I am bi-racial or mixed, however you want to define it. My mother is white (as people call it) and my father is from Jamaica (black as people call it). What I don't understand is why people still judge others on their skin colour. We could do so much more if people didn't judge others based on how they look. My experience of being mixed is a wild one cause it looks like I have a tan. People say my skin colour looks so perfect because it has a tan. When you think of it it is very weird that people discriminate on colour but light skinned people like to have a tan.

Where I grew up I was mostly in a population of white people. So my experience will be different than someone who lived somewhere else. I had two experiences where comments about my skin were made. One time I was in the grocery story buying stuff for my mom. And this lady came up to me and she said "I love your tan" and I said "No it's not a tan; it's my natural skin colour" and she just walked away. And was shocked at the fact that she would just walk away. Then I realized, as I talked about in my other chapter, keeping your power, I couldn't let that one thing effect me; it wasn't that bad. It did happen twice, and at least the other lady said she was sorry before she ran away. I bet there were other cases of when people discriminated against me but you know I didn't let it affect me. I used the tools I explain in this book. That's one of the reasons I decided to write a book. Somehow I figured out how to deal with things that weren't so good. And I thought why not share that with others so they deal with things in a better way?

Don't let anything affect you, even if it is a racist comment; just carry on and make it better. Make your life better. Show them that you can do something better than what they labelled you as. Everyone is a person so why do we need to label them? Just be you. Everyone one else is taken.

People shouldn't be labelled and known as this or that. It could hurt them so much. It could lead them to the point of depression or suicide. Would you want to know that people may be pushed to that because of your actions? I know I wouldn't. I'm going to talk a lot about why you shouldn't be racist. It so important to know why because when you do I'm pretty sure the message will get across and you will stop it. That is what makes this chapter so important.

So tell me; I really want to know why somebody judges someone by their skin colour. I mean it's just their skin colour. It actually makes everyone unique because no one has the exact same skin colour.

If you have a darker skin colour I want you to think of a time when you referred to someone as black. Even if you do not have a darker skin colour I want you to do this exercise. I want you to look around wherever you are and look at something black; now does that look like someone's skin colour?? No because that is a dark shade of black. Now look at something that's white – like a white wall - does that look like a skin colour? No!!! So why do we call it a skin colour? We should call them unique or interesting because it's interesting to see all these different cultures.

Because I live in Toronto I can take the bus downtown to Chinatown, for example, and see lots of cultures. I love going to all those different cultures and trying all that different food which I really love.

Everyone has a different culture/style that they live in. You go to your friend's and the environment is different than your's. That's all, OR it may be the same. People may have a different environment so I don't think we should judge others and that is one of the big reasons that I am writing this book. So people have different skin colours based on the environment they are in, or based on their culture. So why should people judge people on that? We are all the same people living on this one earth.

So if you can get this message: that no one skin colour is the same, and no one should be judged on their skin colour, that would make my day if we were all treated equally.

Because look what happens in the States where kids get shot because just because of their skin colour. I know the media says it but twists the words a little to make it look like they didn't say it – twists it around to make it look like the black person is the problem. The media is so interested in getting a good story that they often don't see the truth in it. Because when I watch stories about kids getting shot for no reason it breaks my heart to see that happening. Because I know that person had a good intention and didn't mean to do anything bad. That should not happen.

I know there are a lot of cases when white people get shot. I'm not discriminating against white people because it happens also. And it also breaks my heart. Why are we shooting? These people may be innocent. I know there is good in everyone. They might be doing something bad and at the time they might not know, but they have good in them.

CHALLENGE

Take a look at everything and see the differences. Remember that so many things are different and that's what makes the world interesting. Write down your observations.

_____

_____

_____

_____

_____

_____

_____

_____

_____

_____

_____

_____

_____

_____

CHALLENGE

Chapter 6
Giving Love

I decided to do this chapter because it ties into all the other chapters. It ties into being yourself because if you give yourself love your mind will register "I love myself." It's brilliant. It also applies to when you're keeping your own power or giving someone else power, because you are giving them love for them. You are giving them love and that empowers them.

When you judge others you are not giving them love. And it also definitely ties into discriminating because when you hate them you are not giving them love. You're not making them feel welcome.

That's also why it's so important because when you give someone love and admiration (another word for love) it makes you feel better. It feeds your soul. I'm not saying love is like kissy kissy love; it may be just giving them a high five. It's a type of love, a type of energy that makes you feel better or them feel better. Or it may just mean clapping for them. It's simple little gestures that will mean so much to others. That's why giving love is so important. It explains to you how much life means to a lot of people.

So when you give someone love it makes them feel better and also makes your insides feel better. There is also another thing. I bet you're wondering why do people do it? Why do you give someone love that you don't even know? The most important thing is when you give someone love it might not be too big to you – for example just saying hi to a stranger – but can mean so much to the other person. I've been in a situation in school when I was feeling down – like getting a question wrong and someone said "Oh Justine just shake it off, you're awesome!" I felt so good inside that someone else cared that I feel better.

It's basically doing something not to get something in return but to make someone else feel better. It makes their day brighter and makes them happier. I don't think you'd want to give someone hate and make them not feel welcome. It's like having a welcome mat at your front door. I love seeing that! It makes me feel so good. What about when you were feeling scared; wouldn't you have wanted someone to comfort you?

EXERCISE

I want to take out a pencil and
paper and write down all the times
that somebody has admired you
and given you love and helped you
in any way. Set your timer on your phone or ipad
and do this for 10 minutes. See how long the list is.

_____

_____

_____

_____

_____

_____

_____

_____

_____

_____

_____

_____

Tell me how these comments made you feel.

_____

_____

_____

_____

_____

_____

I know when I do this the most random comments come up as positive memories.

Yes, simple little gestures like that make you feel better and make their day. So some of you may be wondering how I do that without them thinking "I like them."

I'm going to give you some examples of how to give love without thinking you "like them." It's just simple little gestures like texting hi or seeing someone at the grocery store who may have dropped some coins and you bend down to help them. That's being kind. It makes their day. It happened to me many times that I forgot to bring my money and the nice lady in the line behind me paid for my food. And that made me feel so good that someone else cared about what was going on in my life and noticed what was happening.

That's makes me feel so good inside.

I know I probably explained before why you should do it. Even if it does or doesn't make you feel good inside, your motivation should be to make someone feel good and have a good day.

I want you to take out that paper and pencil and write down one good thing that you will do. Start with just one EVERY day. Just one simple gesture. For example, holding a door at school. Because if someone else is having a bad day you could cheer them up. If it is their birthday you could make them a card/text or call and help them feel good. If you do this with friends that you don't see any more because you moved this will help them feel so special.

I sent some friends a holiday greeting; they loved it and I loved it. Whatever holiday you celebrate, simple little gestures like that are so powerful.

I really hoped you enjoyed this book and learned a lot from it. I really want this message to get across that it doesn't matter how you look or the skin colour that you have. What only matters is what is on the inside. If you can be loving and caring and have a powerful spirit, you will get so far in life.

The world could be such a different place if people understood that skin colour doesn't matter, or what job you have, how rich you are or how old you are. None of those things matter.

I get so inspired to get this book out into the world to show people how I feel and how the world could be better.

A BIT ABOUT ME......

My name is Justine Stenneth, and I am 12 years old. I live in Toronto with my two sisters and mom. I was born and raised in Toronto and I love to travel to Vancouver to visit my cousins Ella and Hayley. I wrote this book because I hoped that it would inspire teenagers and young children to become the next generation of people who make this world even better.